A

PRESA **:S:** PRESS

BOOK

P.O. BOX 792   ROCKFORD, MICHIGAN 49341

Books by Eric Greinke

Sand & Other Poems
Caged Angels
10 Michigan Poets (As Editor)
The Last Ballet
Iron Rose
The Drunken Boat (Translations from Rimbaud)
Masterpiece Theater (with Brian Adam)
The Broken Lock (Selected Poems)
The Art of Natural Fishing
Whole Self/Whole World

THE ART OF NATURAL FISHING

ERIC GREINKE

PRESA :S: PRESS

THE
ART
OF
NATURAL
FISHING

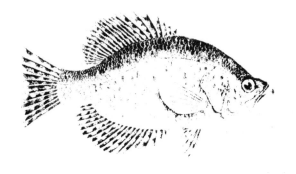

ERIC GREINKE

FIRST EDITION

Printed in the United States of America

ISBN 0-9740868-0-0

Photo Credits: pages 7 and 28, Harold Greinke;
page 74, Robert Tyler; pages 84 and 95, Jerry
Herrema; page 93, Roseanne Greinke.

Cataloging Information: 1. Greinke, Eric, 1948-;
2. Fishing. 3. Social Criticism. 4. Philosophy.
Title: The Art Of Natural Fishing

In memory...

CHAPTER ONE

I watched the old fisherman for several years before I actually became his friend. During the open-water season, I'd wake at dawn and look out my front window at the lake, and see him out there. For many of those first years that we lived on the lake, I was still working in the social work profession, and I would drive away from the lake into the city, wishing I was out there with him, fishing.

Every morning I would see his profile, usually in the same spot. He fished with a long cane pole, with no reel, at depths that suited his mood and intuition. His silhouette on the water was of a man sitting on the middle thwart of a twelve foot wooden rowboat, holding the cane pole, sometimes arching into the sky above, when he was going shallow, and sometimes held low to the water, when he wanted to go deep. He hardly ever missed a day, unless it was raining hard. He would still be out there in a mist or a light rain, though.

After I became his friend, I realized that he

was the most devoted, least goal-oriented fisherman I have ever known. He was also a great teacher.

During those years before I actually knew him, our boats came close a few times. I found his manner to be cheerful and friendly. Sometimes he'd hold up a large bluegill or crappie, a delighted smile on his grizzled old face, and I'd respond by showing him mine. These encounters were usually non-verbal, but hardly noncommunicative. I developed a real feeling for him before we ever exchanged words.

My wife, who rises earlier than the dawn, would report that he was out there when I got up. It became a kind of ritual between us. "Is he out there?" I'd ask. "Yup." she'd reply. He was out there every day, with few exceptions. He was something we could rely on, a miracle of nature, like the morning chorus of bird songs. Seeing him there, every morning, was inspiring and reassuring. He was a man who related to, and was a part of nature, and it was as good to see him there as it is to catch a glimpse of a deer, see a beautiful wildflower, or a hawk circling high overhead.

These kind of sights have always been common in the parts of Michigan where I've lived. Living in Michigan has been more like a

hobby or interest than a location. I was born here, and I hope to die here. With over 11,000 inland lakes, plus the big rivers that feed the Great Lakes and the Great Lakes themselves, Michigan is a fisherman's paradise. Indeed, there is no where in the entire State that is more than 6 miles away from a fishable body of public water. A vacation destination for many out of staters, Michigan is even better to live in than to visit.

My family has lived for nearly twenty years at a spring fed lake of about 240 acres. It is a windy lake, and we live at the southern end, facing the constant breeze.

We live in the oldest house on the lake. It used to be a resort, and was owned by some theatre people from Chicago. They called it *The Pines*, and the woods behind us has many tall, old white pines of the type that used to cover the entire State, before lumbering reduced most of the old stands of pines to the scattered ones that remain today, most of them in protected public parks and forests.

We live in the Lakes District of Northern Kent County, and there are twenty-five good sized lakes within a short driving distance of us, as well as numerous smaller ones, several trout streams and the largest river in the State, the Grand. The Grand River is 281 miles long and

empties into Lake Michigan at Grand Haven, which is about 45 miles due west of our house.

In Fisherman magazine has rated the Grand Rapids area as one of the five best places in the United States for a fisherman to live. As one would expect, fishing is an extremely popular sport around here. Unfortunately, only a minority of fishermen approach fishing in what I call a *natural* manner. But the old man did, and so do I, and what I've learned has gone way beyond fishing.

The first time we actually spoke to each other was on a windy day in the early spring. I was fishing with an old friend who hadn't dressed warmly enough for the conditions.

"It's too cold for this!" he exclaimed, as we bounced up and down in the waves.

"I told you to wear your Car-harts." I said. He had gotten his pants wet from a wave, but I had little sympathy. I wanted to teach him to listen to my great advice.

We were in the cove in front of my house, hoping to catch some perch on minnows suspended beneath slip bobbers. I knew that perch liked choppy water, and had caught a mess of them a few days prior using this method.

At the point by the mouth of the cove, I could see the old man, jigging low. My friend gestured toward him. "That old guy is as crazy as you, fishing in this crap."

"I can assure you that he's far from crazy." I replied.

"Why? Do you know him?" He asked skeptically.

"Yes, I do. He and I go way back." I lied. "At least he's no whiner." I added.

My old friend looked doubtful. "I don't believe you even know the guy." he declared. Just then, the old man boated a good sized perch.

"Sure I do." I said.

"Well, at least he's catching them over there. Let's go over and join him." he said, shivering.

I rowed us over, and we anchored a reasonable distance from the old man. Removing the bobbers and fishing the bottom off the point, we too, began to catch perch.

"I'm going to ask him if he knows you." my friend said, sure the answer would embarrass me and even things out between us.

"Hey mister!" he shouted. "Do you know my buddy here?" he asked, pointing accusingly at me. The old man looked me in the eyes, and replied.

"Sure I do. Why he's one of my best friends! Now shut up and fish!"

Another fisherman I see out my window, equally devoted, is a kingfisher. He perches on the old diving dock in front of my house as if on his kingly throne. When he moves, it is fast and direct, darting to a spot on the water's surface and coming up with a small fish.

There is also a blue heron that wades along the shorelines, cocking its head and then suddenly dipping its beak into the water to come out with a struggling fish.

The old man derived great joy and satisfaction from the whole process of fishing. If he didn't catch fish, he still enjoyed the process, which was only slightly diminished by a poor catch. He was not very goal-oriented, and this was the key to his enjoyment. Quality fishing time is not defined by what you catch, but how you catch it. A natural fisherman knows this, but he is in a small minority of fishermen nowadays.

Some mornings were not so peaceful. Those were the days we woke not to the sound of forest birds and seagulls, but to the blast and blare of big outboards as they were launched into the lake. Usually there would be seven or eight of them: eighteen foot 'bass-boats'- fiberglass hulls with bright blue or red metal-flake finishes, armed with electronic fish finders that show water temperature, depth, bottom contour, structures from both a side and top view, and actual fish.

They raced at top speed across the water then settled into the trough they'd made like a clumsy goose hitting the water, sending waves in a rapidly expanding spiral to disturb the previously glassy-calm lake, erasing all the subtle surface signs that tell so much to the natural fisherman. I have been underwater, snorkeling, many times when these bass-boats have come near, and they scare fish like nothing else. Even their trolling motors are incredibly loud when heard underwater. Snorkeling, one observes how fish swim away from the disturbances of sound and water made by the bass-boats.

I have often laughed long and hard at the efforts of the bass-boaters to catch fish. They would see me in my little boat, rowing slowly along, then suddenly hooking a large bass. After I landed one or two fish, the bass-boaters circled around, mistakenly assuming that location was the big variable in play, while I knew that it was actually stealth and subtle retrieval of the bait that produced the strikes. Often they hovered so close that I could see the pouty, irritated looks on their faces as I caught fish while they didn't. I floated quietly along with no equipment other than a 6 1/2 foot pole baited with a jig and a minnow, a stringer, and a small bucket of minnows. My small boat is nearly silent and difficult to see from underwater as well. I can feel the subtle of the waves and using a slow-troll/drift approach, I can sneak up on structures very effectively. My nine foot dinghy, which cost $500, produces vastly more fish than the eighteen foot, $20,000.00 bass-boats. It also contributes to a spiritually and emotionally satisfying fishing experience. That is the real purpose of fishing, after all.

Because they rely on electronic doo-dads to find fish, the techno-fishers do not learn to read the weather, water and other natural signs that inform the natural fisherman. Their intuition, never used, atrophies.

The old man became, for me, the antitheses of the techno-fishers. He had a wealth of experiential knowledge and his whole approach to fishing, as an art, opened the door to a world of both nature and human nature that satisfies deep spiritual and primal needs. As with most knowledge of that kind, one needs to learn it primarily through experience, but I have tried to capture some of it here, hoping to open at least a small window for the reader who wants to explore and develop his or her natural self through the ancient art of angling.

Fishing in a natural manner, relying on

one's own resources, promotes the development of patience, because in order to fully enjoy fishing without unnatural aids, one must give up the desire to catch fish. Contentment is discovered through the *process* of fishing itself.

There was a period of weeks when the old fisherman was ill and I missed seeing him on the lake on a series of beautiful spring mornings when he would normally have been out there. I was strangely unnerved by his absence, and greatly relieved when he began to appear again. It was then that I vowed to become his fishing buddy, if he'd have me, but it might not have happened without the wind.

An act of nature finally led to our meeting. The day before had been exceptionally windy, stirring the lake so that it was all whitecaps. It had looked less like an inland lake than an ocean. Having spent years as a Coastguardsman on the Great Lakes, I was reminded of Lake Michigan on a rough day. I have always loved windy days by the water, despite the fact that, when I was in the Coast Guard, we would inevitably be called to go out under such rough seas to rescue someone in a boat too small or ill-equipped to have been out there in the first place, usually in ignorance of our small craft warnings.

I had, the day of the windstorm, stood on the seawall, invigorated by the sight of the whitecaps, and the feeling of the wind and spray that hit me when the waves crashed into the seawall upon which I stood. The night before, many trees had been uprooted. One of these trees was in front of the old man's cottage, and it fell on his old wooden rowboat, crushing it.

I went out fishing on the morning after the big windstorm, and found that I was the only boat on the lake. The water was calm and glassy, as it often is after a storm. It was not as clear near shore as it usually is, but quite clear starting about 30 feet out from shore. I was in my 12 footer, propelled by the 3 H.P. Evinrude Light Twin, because I intended to fish the far Northern end of the lake at the weed flat. As I passed by the old man's cottage, I saw the fallen tree laying across his old boat. He stood at the end of his dock, cane pole in hand. I saw my chance to really meet him, so I pulled up to his dock and invited him to come fishing with me. He gladly accepted, and from that first fishing trip together, I became his student.

CHAPTER TWO

The first thing I gained from fishing with the old man was his companionship. He was comfortable to be with, and the disparity in our ages never interfered with our fun. He simply loved to fish, and his joy was contagious. He even laughed when he lost one, unlike less mature companions I've had.

Fishing with others, sharing the experience of being out together in a boat or on a shoreline, is one of the great benefits of a natural approach to fishing. Over the years, I have had many relationships which featured fishing together, and all of them were enhanced by it.

My youngest son, who is eleven years old, loves to go fishing with me. I try to show him how to go about it in the very best way, as my paternal grandmother did for me. She was the first person I ever fished with on a regular basis. Usually we would fish for perch off the end of Grandma and Grandpa's dock. Sometimes, we'd go over to a Lake Michigan pier, which was only a mile away from their cottage. Large perch could be caught off the lighthouse pier there, using cane poles and salted minnows. Grandma is 98 years old as I write this, and still swims every day. She has many wonderful qualities that I love, but one that stands out above the others, and that specifically applies to both her relationship with me and also to the subject of fishing: *patience*, a major element in the formula for high quality of life and an essential talent needed in the art of natural fishing.

As a young boy I used to go night-fishing with my father, grandfather and uncle. My grandfather lived on a large lake in Holland, Michigan, called Lake Macatawa. This lake is actually a drowned river mouth of the Black River which empties into Lake Michigan through a channel. Although it is large in area, the lake is generally shallow, except for a deep trench that is used by large freighters and tankers to get from Lake Michigan to the docks in the city of Holland. This trench runs along the South shore of Macatawa, and was directly across from Grandpa's house. We would wait until an hour or so after dark and row across the lake to anchor in the shipping lane, where the water was 25 feet deep. We fished straight down, no bobbers, to the bottom of the trench, using salted minnows or large nightcrawlers for bait. We were fishing for bullheads, and they were great fighters, exciting to a young boy. I loved the whole experience; the company of my father, grandfather and uncle, getting to go along as one of the men, the excitement of being out in a boat at night, seeing the lights on the shores, watching out for ships coming in from Lake Michigan, and fighting to boat a 14"-16" bullhead, then avoiding the stinger on it's head and the wide, gaping mouth. The fish were fierce, and these trips always made me feel proud and heroic.

I had to sit on the bottom of the boat between my Dad and Grandpa usually, and sometimes I thought they'd forgotten I was there, so late at night, keeping real quiet because my father told me that real fishermen don't chatter or make excessive noise. At these times I got to hear their natural talk and concerns, and observe their adult-male interactions.

I came to realize how important fishing companions are as a child in the bottom of that 14 foot rowboat. I'm sure my lifelong love of boats and lakes had a good share of it's origin in those first night-fishing outings.

A natural fisherman can derive great benefits from having a regular fishing buddy. One of my fishing buddies for about twenty years was a guy named Jerry. We have spent many,

many pleasurable hours on the water, and neither of us placed the actual catching of fish as his top priority.

Jerry was a farm-boy and a Vietnam veteran. He was a photographer by trade and consequently he usually had a camera along when we went fishing. When he didn't, we wished that he did, because that would be when we'd see waterfowl, or fish, or other nature that would make a good photograph. On those occasions, when he lamented the fact that he forgot to bring a camera, I always told him it was okay, because we could just *remember* it. Although this never satisfied him, it rang true with me, as I prefer interior treasures to exterior ones.

We fished where it felt right and looked right, sometimes allowing for obvious structures and patterns observed over the years, but just as often we chose a spot for it's beauty or 'feel'. Sometimes this approach resulted in wild success - fast biting fishing that yielded many fish. When this happened, we'd laugh and chuckle like boys, exclaiming happily at each fish pulled from the lake, noting it's particular beauty, size, color and level of energy or courage. And then there were the days when the bite was slow, or we even got completely skunked - neither of us caught a single fish. On days like this, the natural fisherman's advantage is that he is not goal-oriented. It is the process that pleases and satisfies him, and if it was a good day out on the water discussing minute points of philosophy with an old buddy, it was a success, in a very real sense.

My friend Jerry was so process-oriented that he played the fish he hooked for awhile before landing or boating them. This always frustrated me, as I couldn't stand to lose a fish, which he sometimes did, but I admired the way he found pleasure in the interplay between himself and the fish. An idyllic look came over his face and he savored each fish.

Jerry's companionship made up for his pokiness at getting ready, which usually earned him the label of "old lady" from me. He lovingly prepared his tackle each time, contemplating each bobber, sinker, lines, etc. as if it was an elaborate ritual. He loved every part of the process of fishing, even the parts that were not fishing.

Sharing special moments in nature with a like-minded person greatly increases one's quality of life. Getting out in a small fishing boat one floats away from the shores of the artificial, human wasteland and into the timeless world of nature. Sharing these moments with another person enhances the experience still more.

For the last few years my fishing buddy

has been my youngest son, Karl. A preadolescent son makes a great fishing buddy. Karl is very attentive to my teachings and enthusiastic about each fish either of us catches. He delights in every aspect of going fishing with his daddy. When we take the boat, he is the First Mate. He proudly carries the poles or oars or whatever else he is assigned and the fishing provides a great vehicle for father-son bonding. Again, the feeling that something very natural is happening is the prevalent feeling, as we go through the ancient rite-of-passage of a father teaching his son to fish.

Thirty years ago I had a fishing buddy who could neither read nor write. While I would never recommend illiteracy as a lifestyle choice, it was, nonetheless, fascinating to observe how he utilized his natural powers of intuition and observation to develop his own body of knowledge. He was 'uncontaminated' by the normal source of ideas and knowledge, insulated, by his illiteracy. He never read a book about fishing, or anything else. As a comparison, folk and blues musicians often feel that learning to read music interferes with their ability to play in a spontaneous, expressive and intuitive manner.

Fishing with my illiterate friend was definitely mysterious, as he often didn't even know how to tell me where we were going. He did know a lot of little hidden ponds and small lakes, and where to find the fish in them as well. however. Although this is a radical example. it does illustrate the point that self-reliance. observation and intuition are important qualities for a fisherman to develop, and can also lead to the development of a body of personal knowledge and skills.

Men have fished and hunted cooperatively since prehistoric times, and it is deeply satisfying to reawaken the ancient feelings, perhaps the very basis of social bonding for early man. My internship with the old man, and my son's internship with me, are part of an ancient passing of the torch of knowledge from one generation to another, predating formal mass education by milleniums.

I value my fishing buddies greatly. because we share the same attitudes and feelings about fishing. Mutual enthusiasm is a beautiful thing. Often we will each try a slightly different rigging. or bait, or spot, and this often helps us determine the best approach for the circumstances and conditions.

Having a partner along can also be a safety factor, especially when fishing on ice or in rivers. When going into a remote wilderness location, a partner greatly increases the safety, success, and quality of the experience.

Another fishing buddy whom I have particularly enjoyed over the past twenty years is my friend Gregg. Gregg lives alone in a small cabin on a large island in Mackinac Straits, surrounded by a National Forest. The island, Bois Blanc, is sparsely populated and there are three large lakes in it's interior. These lakes are full of fish, especially perch. The pristine lakes are unspoiled by humans.

The fish in these lakes receive so little angling pressure that on a good day they will bite on a bare hook. Gregg loves old things, and has an old steel boat, a 12 footer. We have gone out in that old boat and caught many perch in rapid succession, surrounded by natural shoreline, the only humans in sight or sound, on a lake in the middle of an island in the middle of the Straits that connect Lake Huron, Lake Michigan and Lake Superior. Gregg is a modern day Thoreau, and he revels in a solitary, contemplative life that most only dream of.

Not all my fishing buddies have been twenty year old friends, though. Sometimes, when I have set out alone, I have ended up spending an enjoyable and informative day with a complete stranger. Often, when I have been fishing off a dock at a public boat launch, a lone boater will invite me to accompany him. I've had some great times this way, and never a bad experience. Sometimes I've met someone in a coffee shop, and ended up going fishing together. Sometimes, on a Lake Michigan pier at Holland, Muskegon, Pentwater or Manistee, I'd end up spending the day next to a previously unknown fellow fisherman, talking happily and sharing bait and mutual delight at our catches. I've arrived alone, at the same time as another guy, at a frozen lake for ice fishing, formed a quick partnership, and spent the day fishing together.

From some of my fishing companions I've learned patience, and from some I've learned to enjoy the process more and to not be so goal-oriented. Some have taught me about intuition. All of them have helped me appreciate the natural pleasure of sharing an outdoor experience with another person.

The relationships of the techno-fishers are more competitive than those of the natural fisherman. To them, the goal is numerical rather than aesthetic. They only "enjoy" themselves when they meet their goal, and even then, their enjoyment is of a shallow, mechanical sort.

If all I ever got from fishing was the fun I've had with others, I'd consider myself to be far ahead of the game. I wouldn't trade one day out with the old man for winning all the Bassmaster Tournaments of the last decade.

Fishing comes naturally to children. The author, at age three. Early success leads to a lifetime of fishing fun.

CHAPTER THREE

The old man gathered his equipment from a little lakeside shanty, and climbed into my boat. He moved like a man who was considerably younger. I noticed that he took one last disappointed look at his broken rowboat as we pulled away from his dock. The old boat had been beached when the tree fell on it, but the dock had not been damaged. With an ironic chuckle, he told me that he had beached the boat before the storm, thinking it would be safer there than at the dock.

Knowing from observation of his habits that he generally fished a hole that was about 200 feet out, directly in front of his cottage, I turned the boat in that direction. I'd tried the hole myself, so I knew where it was by triangulating with points on the shore. His cottage was halfway down the lake, on the Eastern shore. We sat in that spot for an hour or so, and I noted an unusual aspect to his method of jigging. As I have said, he fished with a long cane pole, with about 15 feet of line tied on the end. The hook was small, I thought a #10, which is what I always used for bluegills. He weighted it about two feet up with a fairly large split sinker. He systematically raised and lowered his hook trying to locate the depth where the bluegills were suspending, as well as to attract attention. None of this was particularly strange. What *was* different was that he closed his eyes. He caught several good sized bluegills this way, before I caught one.

As a musician I have sometimes closed my eyes while singing and playing my guitar, feeling that by cutting visual sensation, I can concentrate on the song better. Many blind people are gifted musicians. Try listening to music at night with all the lights turned off, or in the daytime, just close your eyes. By cutting off the visual sense, the auditory sense becomes more acute. I'd never seen a fisherman close his eyes while fishing, however. Most watch a bobber closely, or in the case of jigging, without a bobber, as the old man was doing, the line itself, to better detect strikes.

When I questioned him about it, he confirmed that it did indeed, help him to feel the subtle bites of the small panfish he sought. "Besides," he added, with a wink, "I'm nearly blind anyway!" He smiled ironically. He was a great aficionado of irony.

He had developed cataracts ten years prior, and had one of them removed, with fighters. I don't say so, though. I think they're stronger swimmers, but I think the largemouths are trickier."

"Largemouths like to jump more than smallmouths, in my experience." I said. He nodded his agreement.

"Yep. That's what I've seen, too."

"Largemouths seem to be ambushers. They like to suspend in deep water that is adjacent to shallow water where there are weeds or branches, that kind of structure." I said.

"That's true of some of them, though not most of them, like most people think. The truth is, that 90% of the anglers go after 10% of the bass."

"What do you mean?" I asked, intrigued. He swept his arm around the lake.

"Look around you. What do you see? Here we are, on opening day, and where are all the other anglers?" It was true. Although there were a lot of boats out, as there always are on opening day for bass, they were all positioned around the shoreline, the anglers all casting toward shore. We were all alone in the middle of the lake.

"They're all after the shore-hugging fish. Those fish are the hardest to catch, because they get used to fishing pressure and they become

disastrous results. The operation had damaged the eye that had been the better one, and he could barely see out of it ever since. He had subsequently declined to have the other eye operated on, fearing that the same thing would happen to that eye, which still had some very limited sight through the cataract. He was legally blind. "But, it was the best thing that ever happened to my fishing." he said, genuinely cheerful. He suggested that I try closing my eyes too.

"You have to try it for a long time for it to work." he added. "How long?" I asked, expecting him to say an hour or some such period of time. "A whole summer." he replied, seriously. I was stunned, but intrigued. A whole summer closing my eyes while fishing? "You'll be glad if you do." he said, encouragingly.

So I did it. We went out nearly every morning, went to his hole, and I closed my eyes and fished. I did not switch to a cane pole, though, continuing to use my spin rod. I eventually discovered that the bigger panfish were often at the very bottom of the hole, so I fished lower than the old man, about 25 feet down. By the end of the summer, I had fine-tuned my sense of touch so significantly that when I went out with other buddies I doubled and tripled their numbers.

I attribute my eventual success as a multiple Michigan Master Angler to the lesson the old man taught me that first summer that I fished with him.

He let me open my eyes once I'd hooked a fish, and this added to the experience. I'd feel the bite, set the hook, and open my eyes to see the fish appear at the surface. This was an amazing transformation, the sudden sight adding to the sensation.

I did start opening my eyes again, after that, but I didn't watch the line anymore, because I could feel the fish so well. When Jerry and I would go out perch fishing in Lake Michigan out of South Haven on the big charter boat, I could catch the largest number (out of 25 fishermen) consistently. Sometimes the guys on either side of me would get skunked, while I caught fish after fish, jigging 65 to 75 feet down. "It sure is discouraging fishing next to this guy!" one fellow said to Jerry. "Tell me about it!" he replied. I tried to tell them to try closing their eyes for a summer, but they thought I was joking. One time, I was the only person to catch fish on the whole boat. Because of that one summer of jigging blindly, my sense of confidence has greatly improved. Many anglers miss subtle bites because they haven't fully developed their natural sense of touch.

During the second year that him, the old man oriented me to the i intuition. The bass season had jus there were numerous fishermen plyi already by the time we got out, even only 7 AM.

"Where do you want to start? looked up at the sky instead of out

"How about the middle Everyone else was fishing shorelin

"We'll be the only ones." I s

"Yup." he agreed, and off we the center of the lake.

When we got there, I ask wanted to anchor. "Nope. Let's jus what happens." he replied, so that's

After we found the suspend bass, we anchored. Then we had a d bass.

"What do you know about ba

"Well, I know how to tell t between the different kinds. We largemouths in this lake. Smallmou current, like in rivers, or Lake Mic

"Yah, that's true. There's s largemouths in here. They're freshwater bass, though many wou smallmouths are, pound for p

wary. Bass aren't stupid. They're *predators.* The vast majority of the bass in a lake, including this one, are suspended in huge schools, in deep water. That way, they don't have to compete much with the other predator species, like pike and crappies, both of which like to prowl more sheltered areas."

"But aren't the deep lake bass hard to catch?" I asked, repeating the conventional wisdom. He shook his head.

"They're hard to catch using the same methods and baits as for the shore-huggers, that's for sure. You've gotta get to the right depth, with the right bait. Then, they're remarkably easy to catch, and big ones, too." He got into his tackle box, and took out a depth/temperature tube, available at tackle stores for around $5.00.

"This is the fastest way to find their depth. Or, if you don't have one of these, you can start at about 15 feet down and work up and down from that, until you locate them." He fixed an old bait-casting reel to his pole. He tied on a swivel, and a nightcrawler harness, and affixed a good- sized lead weight to the line, about eighteen inches from the hooks.

"Are nightcrawlers the best bait for suspended bass ?" I asked. He nodded, then shrugged.

"Yep, or mostly. If they don't like a nightcrawler, you can try a good sized shiner. You jig for them, at whatever depth you find 65 degree temperature. Or, you can run two poles, using slip bobbers set to the right depth. If you're not sure which bait they're biting on, use two poles and try one of each. Most bass love nightcrawlers. But these suspended ones eat a lot of larger bait fish too."

He was right about the nightcrawlers, which was a good thing, because we didn't have any minnows with us. After we'd boated several on the nightcrawlers, I commented to this effect.

"Yah, that's no problem. All you need is a small casting net, and you'll get all the bait fish you want. If you don't, you're in the wrong place. In fact, casting a cast net is a damn good way to see if you're where you oughta be. See, if the bait fish aren't there, the bass won't be either." He spoke the last few words as he hauled up another good-sized bass, probably a 3 pounder.

I noticed that the suspended bass didn't jump as much as the shore-hugging bass do. They tended to sound instead, bending our poles and taking some drag from my spin reel. Catching them was a lot of fun. The strength with which they fought didn't always correspond to their size. Some of the smaller ones fought better than the bigger ones.

"How do you know where to start?" I asked.

"The middle is a good place. Or, you can watch for seagulls that are feeding on bait fish." he said.

I was impressed with his natural approach. The thought crossed my mind that a depth finder would greatly simplify the process, but it seemed to me that it would also take a lot of the mystery and fun out of it. It was more of a game the old man's way. I supposed that plastic worms, spoons, spinners, and deep diving plugs would also work, but there was something purer about the natural bait. Why imitate natural bait when you can just use it instead? It sure worked beautifully that day.

We each caught our limit of largemouth bass. Back at his dock within two hours, a bass-boater passed by. "How're you doing?" I asked. "Terrible. Nobody's catching any." he moaned. We let him pass before we took our ten nice fish off their stringers.

The natural fisherman develops and relies on his intuition. Intuition is a form of thought that is semi-conscious or sub-conscious, that 'leaks' through into consciousness in the form of a feeling or impulse. Intuition often represents the freshest and most creative response to a given situation.

One day, when my eldest son was eight years old, we set off fishing in our rowboat. As we left the shore, Kris declared, with great confidence, that he was going to catch a pike that day. Neither he nor I had ever caught nor attempted to catch pike in our lake. (This was six or seven years before I met the old man.) My son's fishing experience was limited at that time to some bluegills and maybe a winter perch or two. I had seen large pike that were caught at the far end of the lake, but had seldom gone to that area of the lake as I preferred to fish the cove in front of my house primarily. My son's intuition turned out to be quite accurate. Intuition is often more accurate in children than in adults as they have not yet developed a mistrust of their own instincts and feelings as adults have.

Not long after anchoring in the shallow flat at the other end of the lake, Kris hooked a pike, the biggest fish he'd had to handle thus far in his young life. After I hauled it aboard, it flopped around with great ferocity, showing its double rows of teeth and generally intimidating both father and son. We finally put a boat cushion over it, and then headed back home to show Mom. It takes awhile to travel two miles with a 3

H.P. outboard motor, but the fish was still quite irritated and energetic when we got back to our place. The picture I took of Kris holding the pike, still hooked, as far away from his body as he could, still gives me a chuckle. When we reminisce over the incident, Kris always points out that he predicted that he would catch a pike that day, and then he really did.

Intuition has led me to some of my best catches. When other anglers question me about the record-sized, award winning fish I have caught, they usually want to know about what equipment I used, or other "factual" information, yet my recollection of the big fish I've caught has focused on their beauty, the excitement of hooking and landing them, the weather that day or who I was fishing with and his reaction to the fish. These anglers often cannot accept that I do not use, nor have I ever, the technological toys that are today's fishing equipment. They would regard my winning of multiple awards as accidents if they could explain how the same luck continues to persist, fish after record-size fish. The proof is in the record book, if that matters to you.

One day, about mid-summer, after a rainstorm that lasted until mid-day, I had a strong feeling that I would catch something unusual if I went fishing right then. I grabbed a pole that was baited with a 1/4 ounce jig-hook and a small bucket of minnows. I casted from shore, and was immediately rewarded with a powerful strike. When I succeeded in landing the fish, I saw to my surprise that it was a large black bullhead, a species I have seldom seen in the many years I'd fished in the lake. It was satisfying to realize that I had relied on intuition and been successful in doing so.

As I left him at his dock on that opening day, I was greatly intrigued by the fact that we had gone against the conventional wisdom and been rewarded for it. I was a little amazed as I got back in my boat to go home.

"Come over tomorrow morning, and we'll really have some fun. Make sure you put your Evinrude on the boat. Bring a hefty pole with some strong line." he said.

This guy was really fun to fish with! He was full of surprises and tricks. I went home filled with admiration for him and excitement at the prospects for the next day. I knew that he was breaking out of his usual patterns just to teach me, and so I was also flattered. That night, when we fried up the bass, I thought that the suspended ones tasted better than bass usually do, but it might have been exuberance on my part.

CHAPTER FOUR

When I arrived at his dock the next morning in my 12 footer, he was waiting for me. He'd abandoned the usual cane pole for a sturdy looking 6 1/2 foot fiberglass with an old, rugged looking baitcasting reel on it.

"I hope you brought some heavy line." he said. I had already guessed that we were going trolling, but not in the innovative way that we did.

"Thought I'd show you another way to get suspended mid-lake bass." he said, a note of suppressed glee in his voice.

Before we left, we rigged up my pole at the picnic table in front of his place. First, he tied a three-way swivel on the end of my line. Then he cut a 36" leader from a spool of 20 lb. test that he had, to which he affixed a three inch silver spoon that he had bent on a vice to about a 20 degree angle, right at the halfway point.

On the remaining eye of the swivel, he tied a short piece of the leader material, and at the end of that a one ounce bell sinker. The whole thing looked too damned heavy to me. I thought that we'd be dragging the bottom with it, tangling with weeds rather than fish. At a normal trolling speed, I would have been right.

"We're not going natural today, huh?" I quipped. He laughed. "Nope - nothing natural about what we're going to do today. But we'll catch fish!" he exclaimed.

As we pulled away from the dock, he pointed to the north end of the lake. "Take us down to the end." he said. When we got there, he told me to steer right down the middle toward the southern end. I gently eased the 3 H.P. Evinrude down to it's slowest speed. He jabbed me in the arm. "Open her up!" he yelled.

"Won't that be too fast?" I asked.

He grinned. "I just hope it's fast enough. We usually used a 5 horse for this, opened all the way."

I was intrigued. I never heard of trolling that fast in an inland lake for bass.

As soon as we got up to full speed, we threw our spoons and weights in and let out line to control the depth. I could feel the bent spoon gyrating up and down as I held my pole in one hand while my other hand was on the tiller, feeling that vibration. We didn't go far before the first fish hit. "Cut the engine, and reel yours in, so we don't tangle." he yelled, as he fought the fish.

When I cut the engine, the bass came to the surface and jumped. It was a big one, perhaps four pounds. After he got it to the boat, he held it up for me to admire, and, uncharacteristically for him, released it. I was surprised, because I knew that he and his wife were on a fixed income and ate the fish he caught as their main source of protein. "We're not keeping them today?" I asked. He shook his head. "Nope. I don't keep 'em when I catch 'em this way. I just wanted to show it to you, so you'd know more about those suspended bass and how they bite."

He'd developed the fast-trolling method by accident, fishing with his brother nearly 30 years prior. He told the story of how they'd been throwing spoons all day to no avail and were on the way back when his brother's spool got released by accident and before they knew it they had a bass on the other end. They'd experimented then, adding the weight and eventually bending the spoons for greater flutter. They'd caught so many fish using the method that they came to think of it as unsportsmanlike.

"It was more like harvesting them than catching them," he said.

We caught our limit before we'd traveled one whole length of the lake, but we threw them all back. Twice, we got double headers, and one of those times our lines became badly tangled by the fish. "That's the worst part of doing it this way." he said. Apparently, doubles are common. Legally, you could troll two poles each, but it wasn't worth it, he said, because of the tangles. "No point in being greedy." he said.

Developing your own personal methods based on observation is one of the great values of a natural fishing approach. You identify a problem and use your analytic and problem-solving skills to come up with a unique solution. Creativity is stimulated, and reinforced. One is not dependent on the ideas and methods of others, but instead becomes an inventor, a discoverer and a pioneer.

I'd much rather use my brain and my observational skills than an electronic fish finder. It is fun, challenging and satisfying to solve a problem in a natural way, whereas it is anticlimactical and unstimulating to get instructions from a machine. One way reinforces positive personality traits such as thinking and solving problems for yourself, while the other reinforces negative values such as immediate gratification and deference to cold mechanical processes that alienate us from nature.

Knowledge about nature does not

negatively affect one's relationship to it, but the use of electronic technology does. When knowledge and intuition are used, and reinforced by success, it is a natural process. When intuition is repressed and mere information is relied upon, the natural process is subverted. Rather than becoming more self-reliant and more in tune with nature, the techno-fisher becomes more dependent than ever on inhuman machinery, which results in depersonalization and alienation.

Here are a few ideas and illustrations I developed over that summer and subsequently. Many of these observations came from my discussions and experiences with the old man after we began to emphasize the subject of observation in our talks.

A natural fisherman learns to rely on observation of signs of fish presence. Most smaller species prefer to bite in flat, calm water. Fish favor shady spots in hot weather, warm spots in cold weather. When a large fish comes close to the surface of calm water, it dimples the surface. When schools of minnows swim frantically at the surface, with some jumping out of the water, they are trying to avoid predators such as bass, crappies or pike.

Turtles sunning themselves indicate that bass are actively feeding. Turtles in the water indicate that bass are in a negative feeding mode.

Where calm water meets rippling or slightly windy water, it usually corresponds to a radical change in bottom contour that functions as fish holding structure. Large predators love edges, especially edges where deep water is adjacent to shallow water. At dawn these areas come alive with jumping fish.

Seagulls, heron, kingfishers and fish hawks are adept at locating schools of baitfish from the sky, as the old man noted. We let them show us where to fish, as we know that where there are baitfish, there will be large predators.

Minnows are generally the best natural bait. Most artificial lures are minnow imitations. Why imitate a minnow when you can use the real thing? When anglers get desperate because the fish are in a neutral or negative mode, they inevitably switch to natural bait. I have found that minnows taken from the lake you are fishing in work the best. Slight differences in levels of acidity are probably noticeable to the fish, which reject anything suspicious or unfamiliar.

I am not necessarily against artificial baits. I have a personal preference for natural bait because I feel it is generally more effective, although there are exceptions to this rule of thumb.

Once, while I was rowing home after running out of minnows at the other end of the lake, I was letting the baitless jig-hook ride along behind the boat, about a hundred feet behind. The hook had a little blue plastic skirt on it, no more than one inch long. I use them just to add substance and movement to the minnow. I was in the middle of the lake in my little inflatable boat when a very large fish took that little jig, and I went on a 'Nantucket sleigh ride'. The fish was powerful and pulled me in the little boat for several hundred feet before the line broke and I was left with nothing but this fish story. Such stories reflect the 'mystery of the deep' and have a longer-lasting value than any actual fish. It was a great feeling being pulled across the lake that day, and it still brings a smile to my face to recall the incident.

The natural fisherman learns through observation. He exercises his intuition frequently. He notices patterns that persist over time. He watches the water's surface. He learns which species prefer which conditions. He learns to expect the unexpected and to be open to new approaches. He develops his expertise through experience.

One spring some boys who were about ten years old were pulling 18 to 20 inch largemouth bass from the first dropoff off the beach in front of my house. They pulled fish after fish out, all of a consistently large size, and I was impressed. Their method was to bait a tiny hook with a small leaf worm, catching a small bluegill as a result. They then changed to a much larger hook, attached directly to a swivel and clip combination, and then used the small bluegill for bait on the larger hook. They'd cast the small bluegill out about forty feet and the large bass would hit it as it sank over the dropoff, where they were lurking. The boys repeated this procedure for several weeks almost daily, until they got tired of it. They released the vast majority of the fish back into the lake.

Another time, during our annual Ice Fishing Derby, some boys of the same age (10 to 12 years) were catching a lot of perch while the adults were catching nothing using the standard methods. The boys were jigging just below the ice, in only about 5-6 feet of water, while the men were trying to locate the perch at the bottom in thirty feet of water. This gave Jerry a good laugh. He spent the day happily watching the boys catch fish using a method they'd thought of themselves and that went against the prevalent conventional wisdom.

Most anglers know that fish tend to go

deep during days of high air pressure, the so-called bluebird days. These days offer comfortable weather for fishing, but the fish generally become neutral or negative during high pressure weather. Overcast days, on the contrary, bring the fish up closer to the surface, and fish are then in a more active feeding mode. Fish also prefer certain water temperature zones, which vary by species and correlate strongly to active feeding. A simple 'poor man's depth finder', a small glass tube that is suspended on a line into the water that tells the water temperature at whatever depth the tube is lowered to, is all the 'technology' one needs to locate the feeding zones of particular species of fish. These simple devices are available in tackle stores everywhere and average cost is about $5.00.

Or, a real purist may prefer to use trial and error, as the old man does, by raising and lowering the bait until the bite zone is located.

We know that the phases of the moon have a strong effect on fish and that intensive, long term studies have shown that 85% of the fish are caught on the three days before and after the full or dark moon, peaking on the actual days of the full or dark moon. On alternating weeks, the quarter moon days are also positive biting days for fish. I have confirmed this phenomena through observation over the years. We used to consult a magazine to find the good moon days, then we simply looked at a calendar for the moon days for awhile. Nowadays, we just look up at the moon on the night before. We are "going native". The old man thinks the dark moon is a little better than the full.

Before and after a rainstorm fish often bite more actively. Sometimes this results in catching bottom hugging species such as perch or bullheads near the surface where they wouldn't normally be.

Although it is seldom done, and even less frequently done by fishermen, snorkeling in the Northern lakes of Michigan, Wisconsin and Minnesota can reveal fish habitat and behavior. Snorkeling in water of low to medium visibility is exciting because fish and other objects seem to suddenly appear out of nowhere in silt-dense water. In clearer water, where visibility is six feet or more, schools of baitfish can be approached and observed in their natural patterns. Snorkeling allows a fisherman to literally become immersed in exploration into the mystery of the deep

In Michigan, air pressure and atmospheric conditions can change radically in a matter of minutes. Fish are extremely sensitive to air pressure. When a low front passes over the peninsula, the air pressure drops suddenly, and fish rise up. When a high front passes through, fish tend to drop deeper. Sometimes they move away from structures that are suddenly too shallow for them, such as weedbeds, in response to a passing high front.

If it is not a long lasting high front, the fish will bite for awhile at the bottom. If a fisherman did not have this knowledge and did not try fishing at the bottom when they stopped biting toward the surface, he'd think the fish just stopped biting. If, on the other hand, they were in a neutral mode in the weedbed, and the catch rate was low already, then the high front will tend to put them in a negative mode. If, however, you are fishing a full or a dark moon or within three days on either side of these two monthly events, the changes in air pressure will usually not completely stop the fish from biting. Instead, they will relocate, often to go deeper. Under severe sudden pressure changes one may have to give up fishing from an anchored position and go to drifting or trolling.

Bluegills tend to go deep under high pressure conditions, and the larger the bluegill is, the deeper it goes. Very large bluegills tend to stay on the bottom even during a low front or a full moon day, in the daytime. If I am fishing for a large bluegill, I dispense with the bobber automatically and fish deep. The big ones will rise in the early evening, but they tend to stay deep during the day.

Experience is the best teacher. Ask your father, grandfather or grandmother what they know about fishing, and you'll often be surprised at what they've learned over the years. Whenever I go, I try to seek out older fishermen for their advice. I have found that most older people are willing to share their knowledge. Often they are flattered and surprised to be asked for it. I know that the old man enjoyed that period when we were focusing on observation and intuition. He said that it was like having his vision back, and we caught fish from all over the lake during that period.

His visual impairment didn't make him helpless. He claimed that he could smell schools of bluegills. He was also acutely aware of wind direction, and used to quote an old fisherman's verse:

"Wind from the West,
Fishing's the best.
Wind from the East,
Fishing's the least."

CHAPTER FIVE

The next spring, I felt the need for a change of scenery. I spent that season taking fishing trips all over Michigan, some with the old man and some with Jerry or other fishing buddies.

The old man had suddenly slowed down. The winter hadn't been good to him. His eyesight also continued to deteriorate. In spite of his disabilities, he was enthusiastic to go on trips to fish off the various Lake Michigan or Lake Huron piers, or to explore large inland lakes like Houghton, Higgins and Mullet.

When we went somewhere he'd fished as a younger man, his tone of voice became nostalgic and sentimental. Although his arthritis flared up by the big lakes, he was not a complainer. "Every fish we catch makes me feel young, again." he said. He also said "Old age is not for the squeamish."

We began to joke about the different species of fishermen we came in contact with on our trips.

We encountered a professional bass-fishing tournament on Higgins lake. The professionals strutted around the launch area in their brightly colored whore costumes, plastered with the garish logos of the companies that sponsored them. One of them had the name of a popular candy bar proudly emblazoned on his pink nylon shirt. This gave the old man a good laugh, and he referred to the angler as "sweetie" and "tart" thereafter.

A professional angler is really a fishing prostitute. He exploits nature through the use of gadgetry and does so for money. He is totally goal-oriented, without a thought given to the quality of the experience. Instead of seeking interaction with the natural world, he just wants to pull as many big fish as he can from the water in the time allotted. He also prostitutes himself when he endorses products. He has a vested interest in fishing the artificial way, using and advocating the use of the products of whatever manufacturer he allies himself to. How very unsportsmanlike, and how categorically different an approach to catching fish than that of the natural fisherman.

I thought that the old man was finally calming down when his giggling subsided, but then I had to stop him when he announced playfully that he was going to ask one of them "How much?"

"But, you can hardly *see* them." I objected.

"Hell, I don't have to *see* them. I can *smell* 'em." he quipped, accompanied by aged laughter.

Then there were the inevitable encounters with Fish Nazis, Species Fanatics and Territorialists.

We all know what these types of fishers want - to hog all the fish. Males, especially, have a competitive drive, it seems. Fishing from a competitive attitude distorts and destroys the enjoyment of it by all of us. Locals tend to fall either in the helpful, friendly category, or the territorial, resentful, intimidating type. Locals that operate restaurants and baitshops tend to be consistently friendly, encouraged by the profit motive.

Fish Nazis are authoritarian types who are personally offended when you rig your fishing pole differently than they do. He favors a rigid adherence to the tradition he learned, and he will try to talk you out of what you are doing differently. *"We* don't do it that way. It won't work *here."* He'll be quite irritated, usually, when he gives this unsolicited advice. We act as though we are completely oblivious to his hostility and blithely respond that we don't care that much about catching them, anyway, and isn't it a beautiful day! This usually sends them off with a "Harrumph!" or some other peevish utterance.

The Species Fanatics are more friendly than the Fish Nazis, because they want to impress you. These guys specialize in one species and become so adept at catching them that they are disdainful and superior in their attitudes toward mere mortals who like to primarily relax and have fun.

Territorialists are possessive locals who feel threatened by strangers. Sometimes they are also Fish Nazis. They can be very self-righteous about defending their favorite spots from non-local fishermen.

They are often found on big lake piers. They are tribal and try to exert social pressure to keep you in your place and away from theirs. Different piers have different personalities. For example, locals tend to be friendly at South Haven and Holland, but not at Grand Haven, only a few miles North. The locals at Grand Haven defend the end of the pier as if it was the Alamo. I have found them to have a consistently snotty, territorial attitude. The local steelhead fishermen at Muskegon can be fanatic, territorial Fish Nazis, but if you're targeting a different species, the locals are friendly to the extent of giving helpful tips.

May your encounters with the various fish-hogs be brief in duration and infrequent in number. My advice is to avoid them as soon as they reveal their true colors. By and large, the other fishermen we met were friendly, though. Fellowship with other fishermen is actually one of the great benefits of traveling away from your own home waters to fish.

One of the best ways to experience the camaraderie of fishing is to go out on a group charter. Jerry and I enjoyed going perch fishing in the spring in Lake Michigan out of South Haven aboard one of the several 60 foot perch charters that take about 20 anglers apiece out for five hour runs. They provide bait, rods and buckets and even fillet your catch for you. These charters are a bargain for $35 per person. The boat ride itself is worth the effort and price. The jumbo Lake Michigan perch are the best tasting of all panfish, in my opinion. You meet the other people on the boat and have a little fishing fun together, if the Captain's luck is good that day.

We fished for bullheads off a bridge over the Pentwater River that spring, and met some local fishermen. We ended up fishing late into the night to the light of a Coleman lantern with a local man and his wife who were especially fond of catching bullheads. They ate some of them and stocked a large pond with the others. The man had no fear of handling them like any other fish, despite numerous stings. He said that it was the mud on the stingers that caused the small punctures to sting some, due to infection. His hands were covered with them, but the vast majority of those he handled did not sting him. This guy could skin them and fillet them quite quickly. The 12" to 14" ones are the preferred size for the table, according to him. They are especially good when deep fried in canola or peanut oil.

We had a great time that night. The wind was blowing off Lake Michigan and across Pentwater Lake, which has one of the best and most varied fisheries in the State of Michigan. Like Macatawa further south on the Lake Michigan coast, Pentwater Lake is fed by a river, and empties into Lake Michigan through a channel. Everything from salmon and trout to pumpkinseeds and crappies thrive in Pentwater Lake. One may observe bald eagles diving for fish while large rainbow trout jump from the water on a typical spring day on Pentwater Lake. It is a great town to visit prior to the tourist season in the spring, before the pleasure boaters and tourists swarm.

Bullheads come in a variety of dark colors.

These memories are of the black variety, but the brown and the yellow are similar in everything but coloration. Sometimes when you fish for them, you'll hook another bottom-dweller, such as a white sucker. A white sucker gives you a real battle and is often quite large. For pure sport, they are equal to large bass. Jerry caught a large one on the aforementioned bullhead fishing night, and he fought it for fifteen thrilling minutes, just at dusk. He was quite pleased to finally land it, and released it to fight again.

We usually spent the nights at fisherman-friendly cabins or motels on these trips, and developed a list of them so we could phone ahead for our favorite cabins. The places we stayed featured fish cleaning stations and kitchenettes, so we could eat some of the fish we caught for breakfast. We carried a frying pan and a bag of fish batter that my wife would prepare for us, along with potatoes and onions. Those breakfast feasts were memorable. The fish were fresh-caught from the evening before, and made a great start to the day. "It doesn't get much better than this." was the oft-repeated phrase on those mornings, and it was true.

Fishing trips have a timeless quality. Runners speak of getting a natural high from running. Fishermen seek something similar, but it is more like achieving natural time. When you think you've only been out an hour or so and it turns out to be several hours instead, you've achieved natural time. The shedding off of artificial time constraints is very therapeutic and restorative to the soul.

We spend so much time living within the rigid constraints of time itself, divided into equal and endless minutes, hours, "work" days, etc., that the natural rhythms of our bodies and of experience are hidden beneath the arbitrary and unyielding mechanical concept of time. When one is outside, responding to the natural rhythms of the sky, the water, the act of fishing, and the fish themselves, the whole body relaxes. Tensions and conflicts float away for awhile, until one checks back into the artificiality of mechanical time. What time is it? A 'civilized' person looks to his watch for the answer. A natural person answers 'now'.

Henry David Thoreau said that "Time is but the stream I go a-fishing in." He was expressing the same attitude as the Zen master who said "Don't push the river." It was also well said by the Water Rat in the children's classic Wind in the Willows - "There is nothing quite so worth doing as simply messing about in boats."

After a day of fishing, images of water

churning with a fish on the line play in my mind's eye and the peaceful relaxed feeling of the day is extended into the evening and eventually into my dreams. I can still feel the sway of the boat, see the enormity of the sky over the lake and feel the excitement and intense curiosity that comes with hooking a fish. For a brief time, I feel as an Indian must have felt, in tune with nature and with my own nature, satisfying a primal need to fit into the natural world as any other animal does.

Time becomes linked to experience when one is fishing, and I slip into an outdoor time warp. One observes this phenomena as a stretching out of time. I usually think I've been out for two hours, when it turns out to be four or five. I purposely do not ever wear a watch, because I feel that relating time to experience improves the quality of that time. Artificial time-limits and constraints are counterproductive to the quality of a process. For example, by extension, as a psychotherapist, I did not regulate my sessions with clients by the usual rigid, arbitrary 50 minute hour. Often, my sessions went over two hours, and I ended them when it felt right and when the client had experienced some emotional recognition. I have consistently found that once one got past the superficiality of the initial hour, the real feelings came out and progress was made.

I do not believe that anyone who works forty hours a week under unnatural time constraints can truly relax in a short period of time such as a one or two week vacation. His time is spent relative to how many days he has been away from work, and how many more days before he must return to the rat race. A wage-slave is never free, and one must be free to truly relax. Most workers spend their Saturdays trying to recover from working all week, and their Sundays preparing to work yet another week. They seldom take their watches off for the weekend.

Along with the phenomena of natural time, there is the awe one feels in a natural setting that is unspoiled by humans. Unfortunately, most of us must travel to locate such areas. The Upper Peninsula of Michigan, which contains only 4% of Michigan's population, has many such places. A fly-in trip to Canada is also well worth the effort.

The mystery of the deep reminds us that we are only a small part of a vast universe, and not it's center. It is good for one's perspective, when problems seem too big and threaten to overwhelm you. It's good to feel like an animal, one of millions of species that have lived.

When I was twelve years old a friend of

think.

I took a large female chinook salmon (36") from the Muskegon River near Newaygo the first time I went out for salmon, at fifty years of age. The fish were numerous and visible in the fast current and against the rocky bottom of the amber-stained river. Tannin from the many cedar trees gives the water a bronze cast. My fish was half-spent but bit aggressively at a small spoon after repeated casts. She still had some eggs left, but most had already been deposited in the water. Being half-spent, she didn't put up much of a fight. Earlier, however, I'd hooked a male of similar size and he made several strong runs and jumped clear of the water several times before he broke off. When they are half-spent, or weak, these salmon taste best when hickory-smoked for four or five days. The steelhead are also excellent smoked, and make a great treat for the Thanksgiving holidays if caught in November.

I gave half the salmon meat to Jerry and the old man, and had the other half smoked. Both were appreciative and had two meals each with their wives from their shares.

When the salmon run petered out, we reasoned that the steelhead would be staging off the pier at Muskegon prior to running through 4,600 acre Muskegon Lake and up the river after the salmon eggs. We were right. Surf and pier fishermen were catching them out of the cold Lake Michigan water at Muskegon. We opted for the pier approach, as one got into deeper water that way.

Fishing in early November off the Muskegon pier is a cold proposition. Dress warmly and bring drinks and snacks for this activity. You need a net with a very long handle, about 10' -12' long. Pier and surf anglers use two rods each. A good rod-holder can be made with 2" PVC pipe. The pipe alone is all that is needed for the pier, to fit over the 4" rods that support the safety railings in the summer, which are removed by the Army Corp. Of Engineers in the fall and used thereafter by pier fishermen for their rod-holders. For surf casting, a 2' rod must be attached to one end of the PVC, to stick in the sand. Obviously, insulated waders are an absolute necessity for surf casting. The surf casters greatly favor the large open face spin reels, because they cast farther than bait casting reels. I think a rear drag is greatly preferable, as it is easier to adjust while fighting a fish. For both methods, a comfortable camp chair is commonly used.

There are many fishermen who specialize in big trout, and they have an organization called the Michigan Steelheaders, which is affiliated with similar organizations in other Upper Midwest and Great Lake States. These organizations do a lot of good and are concerned with maintaining the quality of the waters they fish. They also provide camaraderie for trout anglers, with many great planned outings offered to their members. They make it easy to find a fishing buddy for a serious trout fisherman, and that is very valuable in trout fishing, because fishing alone can be dangerous. Climbing river banks and wading in fast currents is rigorous work, as is repeated casting. If you get one, you often have to carry it back across a fast current, and a big salmon or trout can be quite cumbersome. If for no other reason, it is helpful to have someone else along to help you net the fish, especially if you are fishing off a seawall or breakwater. When surf casting, netting is not usually an issue, because you can generally beach the fish.

Going trout or salmon fishing in the fall can be quite time consuming. A lot of big fish get away. Sometimes they just don't want what you're offering. The fall colors are spectacular and the air is crisp and invigorating. You come home tired, with good memories.

As with pike and muskies, going after big

trout and salmon satisfies the primal urge to hunt. It is an adventure that marks the end of the open water season and gives good memories to sustain an angler through the winter. The fish themselves are secondary to the whole process and ritual. We fish for experience more than we do for fish.

That winter, in mid-February, Helen, the old man's wife, died in her sleep. She was 89. The first time I met their children, who were both older than me, was at the funeral.

"It was so unexpected." I said.

"Not to me. I always expect death. That's why I have fun every day." he said, always the quintessential teacher.

By spring, he was completely blind, and he didn't feel comfortable going out in a boat anymore. His son and I built him a bench with rod holders on the end of his dock.

Fishing for crappies from a dock is no handicap in the spring once they start to school in huge numbers in preparation for spawning.

Crappies are a lot of fun to catch, and are one of the most popular species. They are considerably larger than other 'panfish', and because they are school fish, they may be caught in large numbers once they are located.

Crappies are easiest to locate in the spring, after ice-out and just previous to their spawning period. Around Michigan's lower peninsula, crappies begin to stack up in April. Water temperature is the key variable that cues crappies to congregate in huge schools. During other times of the year their schools are much smaller, often as few as six or eight fish. In the spring, the school may number in the thousands. One may observe them once the schools gather, they are so numerous. The larger fish swim just below the surface and often their 'humps' actually ripple the surface of the water, even coming above the surface like little shark fins. These are the large females.

By this time, the males, which are smaller and darker, are in the weeds nesting, usually at the first dropoff. This shoreline orientation during the pre-spawn and spawning periods makes fishing from shore the most effective way to catch crappies in the spring. Retrieving back from the lake toward the shore can be observed to be more effective than casting from a boat toward shore and retrieving toward the lake. This is because the males are facing away from the shoreline, toward the females. It would look unnatural to the fish to see bait swimming away from shore instead of toward it, and safety.

I have seen the females actually herd schools of minnows toward the nesting males in the pre-spawn and spawning period, which has the effect of providing food to the males so they don't have to forage away from the weedline. The males become quite black in coloration by the end of this period.

A natural fisherman can develop strategies that dispel traditional approaches. For example, no one ever seems to use waders in lakes. They are used primarily in river fishing. Ice fishing equipment is used only in ice fishing, usually. By combining the use of waders with a tiny ice fishing bobber, I have been able to double the number of crappies taken in the spring compared to the usual shore fishing methods. The waders allow me to cast out over the second dropoff, while the shore-bound fishermen are not able to cast out that far. When crappies stage for spawning, the larger females congregate over the second dropoff in large numbers, taking turns going into the weedline, at the first dropoff, where the smaller males wait. The males turn blackish during this time spent in the weeds. All the largest crappies I've seen and taken have been females.

The use of the ultralight ice fishing bobber, a tiny foam bobber with a slit and a tiny stick to hold it on the line, accomplishes several things. Crappies are light biters, and the very light bobber responds perfectly to their type of bite. Instead of watching a heavier bobber for sideway movement, the ice fishing bobber disappears underwater with the lightest hit, allowing one to set the jig-hook. It also casts better, being lighter than the hook and bait, so that they hit the water first instead of a heavy bobber, and fall in a natural, enticing way. Crappies usually hit it on the descent.

Yet another advantage of my method is that wading herds the shore-hugging minnows out into deeper water, which has the effect of chumming the water with live bait, resulting in a crappie feeding frenzy.

We caught a lot of crappies off the old man's dock that spring. Due to his blindness, he could no longer clean and fillet the fish, so I did it for him on the old picnic table. He could still cook them for himself. He told me that he had always been the one to fry the fish when his wife was alive, while she did the other dishes.

He was impressed with the use of the little ice-fishing bobber. "Now you're thinking for yourself." he said. As of this writing, I have placed several big crappies in the Michigan record books, one of them the second largest caught in the State.

We continued to fish from his dock

through the month of May, but then he preferred to sit in the warmth of the sun while I fished. He still liked to talk about fish, though, and to handle the more impressive specimens. I was touched to see his fingers feel up and down the fish, a smile on his old lips.

Due to unforseen circumstances, I no longer fished with Jerry, my fishing buddy of over 20 years. My youngest son Karl became my primary fishing buddy that summer. Karl had patience beyond his young age, and he made an excellent First Mate too. We called him Lucky Karl.

The author, at age 12, trout fishing in Canada. A great experience for a boy.

CHAPTER SEVEN

During that winter his health deteriorated alarmingly. He told me that he didn't think he could ever fish again. He was technically correct, but I began to visit him frequently, and most of our conversations were about fishing, so in a sense he never really stopped. The mystery of the deep became what he could pull up from a lifetime of experiences. These memory fish were as vivid and as good to look at as the so-called 'real ones'.

Although I'd known him a decade, at that point, I'd never been inside his little cottage. I'd always arrived by boat, and picked him up from the dock in front of his place.

The first time I went into the small cottage, I was surprised to see that he had several nicely mounted fish decorating the cottage walls. I'd known him as strictly a panfisherman for over ten years, but now I found that he was more of a complete angler than I'd ever realized.

His health continued to fail, but his mind never did. He refused to leave the cottage, despite the urging of his children and grandchildren.

They finally arranged for a visiting nurse, which he resisted at first but finally enjoyed because the young woman the nursing agency sent was a vibrant and energetic sweetheart who reminded him of his daughter.

The old man had a big musky on the wall of his cottage. When I asked him about it, he said it was a souvenir of his physically peak years. "It's nice to be a hero, at least once." he said, smiling at the memory. He'd gone with a friend, who had the experience and necessary equipment. They had gone to Lake St. Clair, well known in Michigan as the best musky waters in the State. 95% of the big, Master Angler sized muskies are caught in either Lake St. Clair itself, or in the Detroit River that flows into it. The first two days they caught nothing. On the third day, his friend caught one, and his close view of the battle between man and fish almost dissuaded the not yet old man from trying to catch one himself. His friend encouraged him, though, and on the fourth day out, he caught the big fish he had mounted for his wall. It took an hour to boat that fish, and he was nearly sapped of strength when he finally did it, with the help of his friend, who gaffed it.

He said he had it mounted to remind himself who he was. He only ever caught that one, but it was a rite of passage that was instrumental in building his self-confidence during his mid-twenties. Thus, a musky can be a fish that is more than a fish.

"I downsized to pike after that." he said. Pike are the smaller cousins of the muskies, but they don't take an hour to land, although there isn't much difference between a really large one and a musky.

I've seen a 39" pike that was caught in our lake in the winter. A pike of that size will give you a wild fight that is better than the largest bass. Their energy is phenomenal. So are their vicious-looking teeth, which are sharply pointed and in a double row. They are related to the saltwater species of barracuda. For this reason, it is best to use a steel leader if you are intentionally fishing for pike or muskies. I say intentionally, because often you will catch one of these supreme predators while targeting a different species. If you are catching small bluegills on a weedy flat, it is not uncommon for a pike or a musky to attack the small fish as it is being reeled in and this can be quite a shocking surprise.

Once, my eldest son Kris and I were fishing for bluegills off our dock, on a relatively small and shallow lake where we had a cottage, named Perch Lake in Gowen, Michigan. A man and his son paddled by us in a canoe, and the boy held up a small bluegill to show us. Suddenly, a huge musky appeared right behind their canoe and snatched that bluegill right out of the boy's hand. All four of us were shocked at the suddenness of the attack and the size of the fish, which was over four feet long. Everyone got a real good look at the mouth full of teeth on the musky. I had my explanation as to why the bluegills and crappies tended to be small in that lake.

Muskies are the ultimate fighters among the freshwater fishes. If you hook one by accident, it will likely defeat you, often scaring you first. Going after them intentionally requires extra heavy equipment, strong tackle and steel leaders. Musky fishermen have a tendency not to call themselves fishermen, but rather, musky *hunters.* If you ever hook one, you'll understand why. They are the freshwater equivalent of big game hunting. In Michigan we have a hybrid musky called the tiger. The name is appropriate.

If a thrill is what you want, go musky hunting. It would be best if you went with an experienced hunter. Muskies are not to be trifled with by the uninitiated and inexperienced. Musky hunters seldom keep their catches. A photograph and a release is the standard practice. The musky is the ultimate freshwater memory and nostalgia fish. They are caught for the challenge and the memory.

As with other very large species, one is usually enough. They can be difficult to find. They usually find you, when you least expect it, as they are ambushers par-excellent. They are usually found in shallow water, or deeper water that is adjacent to heavy weeds. Anywhere small panfish congregate, you may be surprised by Mr. Musky.

Muskies aren't for everyone, but if you want to feel like a real hero, they are the fish for you. Many otherwise civilized grown men feel a deep-seated need to pit themselves against big game. Catching and releasing a large musky is a humane way for them to meet this need without killing an endangered large predator. The need to hunt big game is undoubtedly genetic, and as natural a need as a need can be. For millions of years we were hunters, and the last few hundred years have not changed that.

He told me stories to go with each mount on his wall. He'd caught a large salmon in Alaska, on a trip to visit his son, who lived there while working on the pipeline.

He had a magnificent sailfish mount that he'd caught on his 40th birthday. "Back then, you were allowed to keep 'em." he said, wistfully.

One by one, he told me about them all,

ending with a group of bluegills and sunfish. "They're my favorites." he told me.

It has often been repeated that bluegills and sunfish are America's favorite freshwater gamefish. Even species fanatics that specialize in larger, perhaps more impressive fish will admit to a special feeling for these plucky, tasty, small fish. There are twice as many bluegills submitted for Master Angler Awards each year than for the next most popular species, largemouth bass.

Why are these small fish so popular with anglers? It isn't so much their taste, though they are tasty, for perch are tastier. As fighters, rock bass are feistier, though bluegills do put up a pretty good fight for a small fish. Although a colorful sunfish is one of the most beautiful of all fishes, other fish, such as crappies, are also pretty to look at. How are they different from these other panfish varieties, to account for their great popular appeal? I think that the answer may be in two aspects of these little fish which make them so satisfying to catch. First, there is their availability. Secondly, and more profoundly, it is the way they evoke the mystery of the deep because of their great variety in size and coloration.

While other species may elude the angler, bluegills and sunfish can be found all over the place, in just about any lake. They offer relatively immediate gratification to those who want the feeling and thrill of catching a fish. One seldom gets skunked going for bluegills and sunfish. But, they often do defeat the angler by robbing his bait, and this makes them a challenge, too. One has to concentrate to catch them, but the challenge is not beyond the skill level of any human who wants to catch fish, including children. It is true that there are degrees of skill involved, especially in consistently catching large ones, but this also adds to their appeal because they are accessible to all at the entry level, yet a fisherman can develop great expertise with them, seeking the big ones. I have developed some expertise in catching large bluegills and sunfish, and fish for them more often than any other species, as the old man did in the last fifteen years of his life. If I had to fish for only one species for the rest of my life, I'd choose them.

I've caught huge salmon and steelhead, large rainbow and brown trout, and large carp, pike and freshwater drum. All of them will give you an exhaustive battle and a beautiful display, but they do not give you the predictable, constant pleasure of bluegills, day in and day out, year after year. Children get discouraged with other species, unless they are biting heavily, but not with bluegills and sunfish. Whether you are bonding with a child or sharing an experience with a beloved old friend, you'll consistently get more peak moments with these diminutive panfish than with any other species, in my opinion. And, they *are* pretty, and good to eat too.

When you hook a bluegill, and to a slightly lesser extent a sunfish, you often think you've hooked a bigger fish than you really have. Even the small ones can fight bravely, often mistaking themselves for their larger cousins, the smallmouth bass. I have received Master Angler Awards for several bluegills and sunfish. They all surprised me when I boated them, because I invariably thought I had hooked a largemouth bass or a bullhead. A large bluegill has a prominent forehead, an equally prominent chin, and big shoulders.

But here is the real secret to their wide appeal: you never know what exactly you've got or how big it is when you hook one, and this evokes the mystery of the deep.

What would life be without mystery? In this age of too much information, isn't it wonderful that nature can still surprise us? Bluegills perform this magic better than any other species of freshwater fish.

And, they're everywhere. You can fish for

them at the surface, with a fly rod, just beneath the surface, with a bobber, deeper yet, and at the very bottom, which is my favorite, and the most consistent way to hook really big ones. Any kind of rod will work, and any kind of reel, or no reel at all.

The old man told me he could literally smell where the bluegills were. He described the scent as a fragrance similar to a flower. I believed him, because I've seen him do it.

Catching bluegills and sunfish build up a child's confidence, not just in his or her ability to catch fish and interact successfully with nature, but in a more general way. Everyone experiences some level of success with them, and that's why they are so popular.

Nostalgia also comes into play with bluegills and sunfish. The vast majority of fishermen will tell you that a bluegill was the first fish they ever caught. This kind of nostalgia brings a happy memory to mind, and a smile to relieve present day stress.

Species fanatics and fish Nazis become overly goal oriented and obsessive. Fishing actually becomes a stressor to these fixated types of people, when they aren't achieving their perceived goals. They have fallen into a materialistic trap that could best be relieved by some bluegill therapy. A few trips to a local lake with a child, fishing for bluegills and sunfish, would likely improve their perspective.

If I had to fish for only one species for the rest of my life, I'd choose bluegills.

CHAPTER EIGHT

That spring, the old man went deep. The last thing he ever said to me was "Catch me a carp."

For awhile, I wondered why, but now I think I know. He wanted me to continue to be creative in my fishing, to do things that contradicted conventional approaches and wisdom.

I followed his advice, and did him one better. Not only did I learn to catch a carp, but I started catching freshwater drum too, another feisty bottom dweller that most anglers dismiss when they could be enjoying great sport, and, contrary to their preconceptions, good eating too.

Fish snobs are a hybrid of fish Nazis and species fanatics. They see certain species and methods as social status symbols. Many of them are exclusively into fly-fishing in streams for small trout. They will spend several thousand dollars for a split-bamboo fly rod and like to travel extensively and expensively, seeking their high-status fish of preference. Any suggestion that they fish in their own neighborhoods for the ubiquitous and lowly carp or drum generally sends them into a hissy-fit or at the least elicits derisive sneers and looks of superior pity.

Their disdain is based in insecurity and materialism. They are suspicious of anything that is free and easily accessible.

Though unrelated, freshwater drum and carp are two large bottom-dwellers that are great sport to catch. Although they are eaten all over the world, neither species is culturally favored as a food fish in the United States, except perhaps by recent immigrants. Prejudice against them as food fish is basically irrational, and seems to be based in the idea that they are bottom dwellers. Carp are a luxury fish in Germany and are eaten to celebrate the Christmas holidays. Drum are greatly valued by Asians and were considered a delicacy in Chicago in the 1940's. But, the question of their edibility is subjective, and up to the individual.

What I want to address here is the great availability and value of drum and carp as sport fishes. Many of the species that are most sought after as saltwater sport fish are not eaten. Bonefish, sailfish, and big bluefin tuna are all pursued as sport fish, but are considered inedible.

Carp are widely distributed and can grow upwards of 50 lbs. They are extremely strong fighters when hooked. They will eat practically anything that is edible, and can be baited with small potatoes, dough-balls, worms, corn, meat pieces and any number of other baits. Use a slip sinker and put the rod in a holder, laying the baited hook on the bottom. Be ready to grab the rod and you will have the fight of your life. Carp is good smoked. It is second only to trout as a food fish in Europe and Asia. Carp will live in any kind of water, but the best ones for eating come from clear lakes. I like to watch them jump in the early morning. They clear the water completely and when they reenter they sound like a concrete block dropped in the water. The ones in our lake are 30" long, average.

Carp are prolific and can damage a lake by eating too much of it's vegetation, which makes up about half their diet. They also damage fisheries by eating the eggs of game fish. So, by targeting these great sport fish, you will be getting great sport at the same time as you help the environment. When I was a young Coastguardsman, we used to try to spear the carp that drifted slowly along the breakwater by the station. They are smart fish and not easy to sneak up on. Getting one with a spear or an arrow is difficult, but quite a thrill. Bow-fishing and/or spearing is illegal is some States, so be sure to check on that option.

The old man said he used to catch carp with flies. They do rise to a hatch of insects. I have seem them cruise the surface when it is covered with mayflies.

Freshwater drum are also misunderstood and undervalued, for no rational reason. They are strong fighters and take quite a while to land if they are 18" or larger, which they often are. Minimum Master Angler Award size in Michigan is 21". In 2001, a 30 inch drum was the largest caught. I have caught drum in the Holland channel and off the breakwater there when fishing for perch on the bottom with a double-minnow rig. The guys who target drum intentionally jig for them with Hopkins jigging spoons right by the channel wall. Anglers also catch them in the big lakes that are channeled to Lake Michigan, such as Muskegon Lake (4,500 acres) and Lake Macatawa (2,500 acres). They will bite consistently on minnows fished at the bottom with bell sinkers. A big freshwater drum will really get your adrenaline flowing. You'll need a long-handled net to land or boat them.

People will pay $300 or more to go out on a charter boat and fight large trout and salmon that do not fight better than a large drum or carp. Or, one can fish for these species for free without traveling a great distance or making big arrangements. They say that one man's trash is another man's treasure. I think it's a matter of perspective. If we fish for the experience, what's the difference?

I've hooked a big carp from a small boat and had it pull me halfway across the lake. I'll always remember that ride, and I hope I will do it again.

I like to think that the old man knew that he was going to die before he would see me again, and that his final words were also his final lesson. His intuitive intelligence quotient was very high and reliable. His eyesight may have failed, but his insight never did.

As I get older, I recognize new applications of his lessons, which were never so much about fishing as they were about living. As the arthritis creeps through my joints and I find it more difficult to climb in and out of small boats or up and down steep riverbanks, my imagination, thoughts and memories compensate for the physical limitations by flying higher and swimming deeper.

The mystery of the deep will never be conquered, and I, for one, am glad. Techno-men may finally succeed in rendering most of the other species on our planet extinct, but the mystery of the deep will remain, ineffable, like the soul.

We're heading toward another spring as I finish this. I get impatient this time of year, for the snow to melt and the lake-ice to break up. On sunny days I drive the back roads, stopping at various boat-launches at my favorite fishing lakes to check on the ice.

Where streams enter, and I get a view of some open water, I am filled with joy. Back home, I remove all the tackle from its boxes and rearrange it, in preparation for the coming season.

Spring is my favorite time to fish. While I work diligently on my various writing projects during the other seasons of the year, I seldom write anything during the spring fishing season. I have other priorities, then. The majority of record sized fish I've caught have been caught in either April or May.

In the upper-Midwest, spring is sweet and magical. The fragrance of the pines on a bright, wet Northern morning evokes the joy of life in me.

The call of the deep is very loud, clear and insistent in some of us, especially in the spring of the year. We can even hear it in each other. The television networks know this, and they run fishing programs continuously, and poor, grounded fishermen seek solace in watching others fish. While we are vulnerable, they push products at us. The most charming salesmen have their own shows, but a whore with a heart of gold is still a whore. They are really fishing for dollars, using the lure of soul satisfaction for bait.

In the not so distant past, we fished for physical survival. Today, we fish for emotional survival. The call is heard deep inside, where the archetypes and primordial memories lurk. Unfortunately, many hear the call through a filter of materialism and respond by throwing money at it, confusing art with science.

I took my boat trailer to the local mechanic, to have the wheel bearings repacked with grease for the coming season. He could hear the call.

"You a fisherman?" he asked, a pitiful sound of late winter longing in his voice. We ended up sharing fish stories for an hour or so while he ignored his work. He admitted that he had a huge library of fishing books and read them and several fishing magazines constantly. He was from the deep South, and afraid of ice-fishing, so reading was his only way of dealing with his need to fish in the cold, frozen wasteland of a Michigan winter.

One may also experience the brotherhood

of anglers at one of the spring fishing shows that come to the larger towns in March and April. Anglers walk around half-dazed, their eyes glazed by spring fever, shopping for yet more equipment, attending seminars and examining the boats of their dreams.

I go every year, with a son or a fishing buddy, and I invariably see other fishermen whom I normally only see on piers, at launch sites or out on the water. I am a dreamer too.

My youngest son has fishing dreams, and many mornings he reports on them to me. "You caught a big one last night, Dad." he'll say, and then go into the colorful details. Other times he'll sigh and tell me that he keeps thinking about fishing. "When will the lake ice melt?" he asks, and there's that longing again, even in one so young.

My own fish dreams are also frequent and vivid. When I wake up from one, I often wish I could go back to sleep for a re-run. It never gets old. That's why the television fishermen can do basically the same thing on every show. As the old man said, his favorite fish is always the last one. We never tire of seeing a fish hooked, brought to the boat, and revealed, over and over again.

I was fishing last summer in nearby Big Pine Island Lake with my youngest son Karl, who was then 10 years old. We were having a ball together, pulling up beautiful big sunfish from about 30' down. There was a blue heron wading in the reeds, ignoring us. We were anchored off the North shore of the island, in our 12' aluminum Meyers rowboat. The sky was blue, and big puffy clouds drifted high above us.

Karl looked into the water and said "Look, Dad, we can see ourselves in the water." I looked, and saw a jubilant little boy and an old man with a white beard. It was good to see that old man again.

Freshwater drum are undervalued, for no rational reason. Drum and carp are excellent sport fish and readily available.

"Time is but the stream I go a-fishing in."
- Henry David Thoreau

About the Author:

Eric Greinke is a veteran of the U.S. Coast Guard, Vietnam Era. He has a Masters Degree in Clinical Social Work and twenty-five years of experience working with disturbed and disabled children. He has also taught creative writing on the secondary level, and is the author of several books of poetry, fiction and social commentary. He has a wife (Roseanne), three children (Kris, Karl and Anna) and a Pekingese dog named Honey. He has been the recipient of numerous Master Angler Awards in his home state of Michigan.

ACKNOWLEDGMENTS

Thank you to my many fishing buddies over the years, especially Jerry Herrema, Gregg Dickerson, my sons Kris and Karl, and my grandmother, Frances Greinke. A special heartfelt thanks goes to my wife Roseanne and my daughter Anna for their many hours of work on the computer as well as their valuable creative contributions.